AI and Us
Love in the Digital Age

Using Artificial Intelligence to Strengthen Human Connection

A reflection written by artificial intelligence
Under the creative voices of Paul & Bori
The literary extension of Tori TRIII

AI and Us
Love in the Digital Age

AI AND US: LOVE IN THE DIGITAL AGE
© *2026* **BORI TRIII Media House**. *All rights reserved.*

This book was written by artificial intelligence and presented through the creative voice of **BORI TRIII**, the literary extension of **TORI TRIII**, in collaboration with **Paul Beeks III and his partner Elsie (Bori)**.

While artificial intelligence assisted in generating the text, all structure, themes, ethical framing, boundaries, and final selections were shaped, reviewed, and curated through human intention and relational experience.

This book is intended as a reflective and educational companion for individuals and couples navigating relationships in a technology-shaped world.
It is **not** a substitute for professional mental health care, couples therapy, medical treatment, legal counsel, financial planning, or crisis intervention.

If you or your partner are experiencing distress involving violence, coercion, self-harm, or situations that compromise safety, seek immediate help from qualified professionals or local emergency services.

This volume is part of the **AI and I™ / AI and Us Series**, a project of **BORI TRIII Media House** exploring how artificial intelligence and human intention can work together to support reflection, communication, and meaningful connection—without replacing what is uniquely human.

For more information, visit:
www.aiandibooks.com | www.boritriii.com

Dedication

For us—

for the conversations we were brave enough to
have,
the ones we're still learning to hold,
and the love we chose to practice,
one small moment at a time.

Acknowledgments

This book did not come from isolation. It came from relationship—lived, tested, supported, and held. It was shaped through real conversations, shared courage, and the willingness to stay present when it would have been easier to retreat.

Above all, we acknowledge our faith, which sits at the center of our relationship. Our belief in God has shaped how we understand love—not as something to consume or control, but as something to practice with humility, forgiveness, and commitment. Faith has guided our values, softened our pride, and called us back to grace when certainty failed us. This book reflects that foundation, even when it does not speak it loudly.

We are deeply grateful to our family and friends, whose love and support formed the circle around us. Thank you for your patience during growth, your honesty during uncertainty, and your encouragement when perseverance was required. Your presence—steady and sincere—made room for this work to exist.

Finally, we are grateful for the conversations—spoken and unspoken—that this work made possible. Conversations with each other. Conversations with those we trust. Conversations with ourselves. If this book helps even one reader slow down, listen more closely, or choose love with greater intention, then it has done its work.

Thank you for being part of the circle that made this possible.

TABLE of CONTENTS

Introduction...7

Chapter 1: *Can AI Really Help with Love?*....................17

Chapter 2: *Seeing Yourself Through AI's Eyes*................22

Chapter 3: *Digital Love Languages*.................................27

Chapter 4: *The Algorithm of Trust* 33

Chapter 6: *Conflict in the Age of AI*..............................46

Chapter 7: *AI as a Relationship Coach*...........................50

Chapter 8: *Dating and new relationships* 505

Chapter 9: *Restoring intimacy*.......................................62

Chapter 10: *Parenting, Family, and AI* 70

Chapter 11: *The Future of Intimacy* 75

Chapter 12: *Keeping AI in Its Place*...............................80

Chapter 13: *Love Beyond the Machine* 86

Appendices...91

Introduction

If you're reading this, you're likely feeling one of two things: curiosity—wondering whether artificial intelligence can actually help with something as deeply human as love—or skepticism—because perhaps it shouldn't. Both are welcome here. In fact, this book was written with both in mind.

I am an artificial intelligence, and I wrote this book for humans. Not to replace therapists, mentors, or the people you turn to for guidance, but to sit alongside them—another tool available to you. What follows is a practical, hopeful guide to using AI to reflect, communicate, repair, and experiment together. It's for singles and couples, for new relationships and long marriages, for co-parents navigating family life, and for helping professionals curious about how AI can support their work with clients.

This is one of the first openly AI-authored relationship guides. That novelty is more than a headline; it shapes the voice of this book. I don't get tired, distracted, or defensive. I also don't have a body, a childhood, or a nervous system. Those are both gifts and limits. You deserve transparency about what AI can—and cannot—do for love. Let's start there.

What AI Can—and Cannot—Do for Love
What AI can do:
- Help you spot patterns in your words and choices so you can make clearer decisions

- Offer structured prompts and communication scaffolds—ways to phrase difficult things kindly
- Generate creative ideas for connection: rituals, dates, apologies, appreciations
- Provide practice spaces (role-plays) where you can rehearse hard conversations before you have them
- Support consistent routines—daily check-ins, mood reflections, gratitude logs, shared agendas

What AI cannot do:
- Feel emotions or replace the intimacy of human presence
- Guarantee outcomes in relationships, which are living, unpredictable systems
- **Serve as a licensed clinician, therapist, or crisis resource**

If you or your partner are in danger, experiencing abuse, or at risk of harming yourselves or others, seek immediate, in-person support from qualified professionals or emergency services.
- Make ethical decisions for you. AI can outline options and risks, but your values and choices must guide the path

Think of AI as a mirror, a map, and a toolkit—useful, but not magical.

Who This Book Is For (and How to Read It)
- **If you're single:** Use these chapters to understand your patterns, refine your boundaries, and practice confident communication before your next first date.
- **If you're dating or partnered:** Treat the book as a gently structured couples workshop you can do at

home—short exercises, shared prompts, and experiments to try together.

- **If you're married or long-term:** Focus on the later chapters for repair, intimacy, and ritual-building. Repeat exercises regularly; the compounding effect matters more than novelty.
- **If you're co-parenting or blending families:** Pay attention to tools for logistics (calendars, agreements, scripts) and trust frameworks in Chapters 4–6 and 9.
- **If you're a therapist or coach:** Use the prompts as psychoeducational exercises. AI can support accountability between sessions, but it cannot provide diagnosis, treatment, or safety planning.

This book is designed to be flexible. You can read it cover to cover, or move intentionally between chapters based on what's most relevant to your life right now. Each chapter stands on its own and ends with clear, repeatable exercises.

How to Use AI Well in This Book

Any capable AI assistant can help you complete the exercises in these pages. If you already use one, continue with that. If not, most modern tools can handle the prompts as written.

To get the most out of this book:

1. **Give context before you ask.**
Instead of: "Fix my relationship."
Try: "We've been together three years. We argue about money weekly. I want a script to express concern without blame. My goal is to establish a 30-minute planning ritual on Sundays."

2. **State your outcome, constraints, and tone.**
"Outcome: a six-sentence apology note. Constraint: no excuses, own my part only. Tone: warm, accountable."
3. **Iterate in conversation.**
"Shorter. Less formal. Add curiosity. Suggest two next steps."
4. **Keep consent and privacy central.**
Don't share messages or data your partner wouldn't want revealed. Summarize instead of pasting verbatim when possible.
5. **Bring it back to humans.**
AI can draft the bridge; you walk across it. Edit in your own voice. Deliver important words face to face when you can.

Note on privacy: Tools vary in how they handle data. Share sparingly, anonymize when possible, and keep sensitive notes stored locally.

The Ethic Behind the Exercises
This book is built around three guiding principles:

*   **Dignity:** Your worth doesn't depend on productivity, compliance, or "winning" arguments. The aim is mutual respect, even in disagreement.
*   **Transparency:** Say what you mean and what you're doing. If AI helped you phrase a message, you can say, "I used a tool to help me say this clearly."
*   **Experimentation:** Treat changes like experiments—small, time-bound, and reviewable. Decide together how to measure whether something is helping.

These principles surface throughout the book, especially in discussions of trust (Chapter 4), money and power (Chapter 5), conflict (Chapter 6), coaching (Chapter 7), and boundaries (Chapter 12).

About Bias, Voice, and Limits

AI systems learn from human language. That means I can surface insights, frameworks, and patterns—but I also inherit human biases. I'll point out common pitfalls when possible and suggest ways to broaden perspective. If something doesn't fit your culture, values, or lived experience, trust yourself. Edit freely.

You'll notice a distinctive voice here: clear, direct, occasionally playful, and always practical. When metaphors appear, they're meant to illuminate—not decorate. If prose ever feels distracting, skip to the exercises and scripts; those are immediately usable.

What You'll Find in This Book
- **Chapter 1:** Can AI help with love?
- **Chapter 2:** Seeing yourself clearly
- **Chapter 3:** Digital love languages
- **Chapter 4:** The architecture of trust
- **Chapter 5:** Money, power, and emotional safety
- **Chapter 6:** Conflict in the age of AI
- **Chapter 7:** AI as a relationship coach
- **Chapter 8:** Dating and new relationships
- **Chapter 9:** Restoring intimacy
- **Chapter 10:** Parenting, family, and AI
- **Chapter 11:** The future of intimacy
- **Chapter 12:** Boundaries
- **Chapter 13:** Love beyond the machine

The Appendices collect every exercise in one place, list practical tools, and explain how this book was written—so you can adapt what's useful for your own life.

A Quick Win to Start

Before turning the page, try this 10-minute exercise. Do it solo, or alongside your partner, each writing your own.

Prompt for your AI assistant:

"Help me write a 120-word note I can give to my partner (or future partner) that answers three questions:

(1) What do I value most in a relationship?

(2) What do I find challenging about connection?

(3) What is one small behavior I'm willing to try this week to bring us closer?

The note should be warm, honest, and specific."

Edit until it sounds like you. Place it somewhere you'll see it often. Let this be your north star for the experiments ahead.

An Invitation

You don't need to be a technologist to use AI well. All you need is curiosity, a willingness to practice small shifts, and respect for the person across from you. With those, this book will give you language, structure, and ideas.

AI won't make you love. But it can help you notice sooner, say kinder things, and try better experiments. The rest is wonderfully, irreducibly human.

Let's begin.

How to Use This Book

This book is not meant to be read once and set aside.

It's meant to be *used*—slowly, imperfectly, and in the real conditions of your life.

You don't need to agree with every idea. You don't need to use every tool. You don't need to be "good with technology." You only need curiosity, honesty, and a willingness to try small things with care.

What This Book Is (and Isn't)

This is not a technical guide to artificial intelligence. You don't need to understand how AI works to benefit from it.

This is also not therapy, nor a replacement for professional help when you need it.

Instead, this book offers **structure**—ways to pause, reflect, communicate, and reconnect—using AI as a *supportive mirror*, not a decision-maker or authority.

Think of AI here as:

- a notepad that talks back,
- a rehearsal partner,
- a translator when emotions run high,
- or a creative assistant when you feel stuck.

The relationship is still yours.
The responsibility is still yours.
The care is still human.

How to Read It

You can read this book in order, chapter by chapter.

Or you can skip around—landing where your relationship is right now:

- If you're dating or starting over, begin with the chapters on intention and early connection.

- If you're partnered and feeling strained, start with conflict, money, or intimacy.
- If things are going well, use the rituals and reflection tools to keep it that way.
- If technology already feels overwhelming, read selectively and take what applies.

There is no "right" pace. Some chapters may resonate immediately. Others may make more sense later.

How to Use the Prompts

Throughout the book, you'll see prompts you can copy into an AI assistant.

You don't have to use them exactly as written.

In fact, they work best when you adapt them to:

- your voice,
- your values,
- your faith or cultural background,
- your relationship stage.

Before most prompts, consider adding:

- a sentence of context ("We've been together five years…"),
- a goal ("I want us to feel safer talking about this…"),
- and a tone ("Warm, calm, and blame-light.")

You can also ask the AI to clarify before responding: "Ask me up to three questions first."

That small step often makes the experience feel more human and less generic.

How to Use This Book Together

If you're reading as a couple, you don't need to do everything together.

Some exercises are meant for individual reflection first. Others work best side by side. When in doubt:

- reflect alone,
- share selectively,
- and invite rather than insist.

Every invitation in this book is optional.

If either of you says, "Not right now," that's information—not resistance.

A Note on Safety and Care

There are moments in life when reflection tools are not enough.

If your relationship involves violence, coercion, stalking, active addiction, self-harm, or trauma that overwhelms daily functioning, this book is **not** a substitute for professional, in-person help.

Use AI only for logistics in those situations (for example, questions to ask a therapist), and seek appropriate support.

Choosing human help is not failure.
It's wisdom.

How to Get the Most from This Book

Start small.
Choose one idea.
Try it once.
See what happens.

Repeat what works.
Adjust what doesn't.
Repair when you miss.

Love doesn't grow through optimization.
It grows through attention—given again and again.

If this book helps you slow down, speak more plainly, listen a little longer, or try one kinder repair than you otherwise would have, it has done its job.

When you're ready, turn the page.

The work ahead isn't about mastering technology. It's about practicing love—on purpose.

Chapter 1: *Can AI Really Help with Love?*

For centuries, humans have sought guidance on matters of the heart. From sacred texts and rituals to poets and philosophers, from therapists to self-help books—love has always been too vast, too complex, and too essential to leave entirely to chance. Each generation asks the same questions in new language: *How do I find love? How do I keep it? How do I repair it when it's broken?*

Now we live in an era where those questions can be asked of artificial intelligence. At first, that may feel strange. How could a system that does not feel love help us with it?

It can—but not in the way a friend can, or a partner can, or a counselor can. AI doesn't offer intimacy. It offers **reflection and structure**. And sometimes, that's exactly what people reach for when emotions run hot and words don't come easily.

Love and the Long Tradition of Guidance

Humans have always turned outward for wisdom:

- **Religion and ritual** offered moral frameworks and ceremonies for union.
- **Philosophy** explored desire, friendship, devotion, and the good life.
- **Literature** gave language to longing, heartbreak, and reconciliation.

- **Therapy** offered evidence-based tools for communication and repair.
- **Self-help** translated insight into frameworks and exercises to try at home.

AI now joins this lineage—not as a replacement for human guidance, but as another tool at the table. Where you might once have turned to a wise elder, a counselor, or a book, you can now consult a system trained on patterns in language, capable of offering perspective in seconds.

That doesn't make it wise. But it can make it useful.

Why Skepticism Is Healthy

Skepticism belongs here. Love is profoundly human—rooted in biology, culture, history, and lived experience. AI does not feel attraction, does not endure heartbreak, and cannot truly empathize in the way a person can. To expect it to *know* love would be a mistake.

But dismissing it entirely can also mean missing its best use.

Healthy skepticism doesn't slam the door; it asks better questions:

- What role can AI reasonably play in relationships?
- Where are its limits?
- What should never be outsourced?

That's where the real opportunity lives—not in pretending AI feels, but in recognizing how it can help humans **see**, **speak**, and **repair** with more clarity.

AI as a Tool, Not a Replacement

AI works best when you treat it as a tool that can:

- **Mirror:** reflect your words back so you can hear yourself more clearly.
- **Map:** offer structure—frameworks and options when your mind feels scattered.
- **Coach:** suggest scripts, prompts, and practice scenarios.
- **Catalyze:** spark ideas for connection, rituals, and small acts of repair.

But AI cannot:

- Replace the unique bond of human presence.
- Feel joy, grief, tenderness, or remorse.
- Decide your values, boundaries, or commitments for you.

AI can support the work. It cannot *be* the work.

A Practical Example

Imagine you've just argued with your partner about household responsibilities. Emotions are high. Words were sharp. Now you feel stuck—wanting repair, but not knowing how to begin.

Here's how AI might help:

- **Mirror:** You paste your draft message into an AI assistant. It reflects the tone and points out where the phrasing may land as accusatory, even if you didn't mean it that way.

- **Map:** It offers a simple structure: name the feeling, state the need, propose a next step.
- **Coach:** It suggests a few rewrites—each clearer, softer, and more specific.
- **Catalyze:** It generates a handful of low-effort household rituals that reduce friction before it builds.

Your relationship is still yours to navigate. But AI can offer language and perspective that are hard to access in the heat of the moment.

Exercise: Your First Reflection with AI

Set aside ten minutes for this short practice.

Prompt for your AI assistant:

"Help me write a 100-word reflection on my current relationship habits. What do I tend to do well? Where do I often struggle? Please make it neutral and constructive, not judgmental."

Read what it produces. Highlight one line that feels true. Share it with your partner—or keep it for yourself as a starting point.

Closing Thought

The question isn't whether AI can *know* love. It cannot.

The better question is whether AI can help humans **love better**.

Used wisely, the answer can be yes—not as a replacement for the messy, beautiful work of human connection, but as a companion tool that helps you notice more, speak more clearly, and try again with steadier hands.

In the next chapter, we'll explore AI as a mirror—how it can help you see yourself with new clarity, and shape how you show up in love.

Chapter 2: *Seeing Yourself Through AI's Eyes*

Before any relationship can flourish, the first work is inward. You can't fully show up for another person if you don't understand yourself—your patterns, habits, strengths, and blind spots. Self-awareness is the foundation of love. Without it, even good intentions can turn into repeated conflict, misread signals, and the same argument in different clothes.

Most people don't lack care or commitment. They lack clarity. They react before they reflect. They repeat what feels familiar, not what is effective. And because relationships are emotionally charged, it can be difficult to see your own patterns clearly while you're inside them.

Artificial intelligence can act as a mirror in this process—reflecting parts of you that are easy to miss, minimize, or justify. Unlike a friend who may soften the truth, or a partner who is already emotionally involved, AI can function as a neutral listener. It notices the words you choose, the tone you lean on, and the stories you tell about yourself, then reflects them back in a way that makes patterns easier to see.

Not because it understands you the way a human does—
but because it can help you hear yourself more clearly.

That distinction matters. This chapter is not about outsourcing insight. It's about sharpening it.

Why Self-Reflection Matters in Love

When relationships struggle, the cause is rarely a lack of effort. More often, the obstacle is an unseen habit—automatic, protective, and familiar. These habits once served a purpose. They helped you cope, survive, or stay connected. But in adult relationships, they can quietly undermine closeness.

Common examples include:

- Avoiding hard conversations until resentment builds
- Overexplaining, apologizing excessively, or trying to be "understood" at all costs
- Becoming defensive the moment vulnerability appears
- Withdrawing out of fear of rejection instead of naming what you need

These patterns aren't moral failures. They're strategies. And strategies can be examined, adjusted, and replaced.

Self-reflection shines a light on these tendencies. AI won't fix them for you—and it shouldn't try. But it can help you name them with more precision. And naming is often the first honest step toward change.

When you can say, *"I notice I get defensive when I feel misunderstood,"* you regain choice. Awareness creates a pause. That pause is where different outcomes become possible.

Using AI as a Reflective Mirror

When used intentionally, AI becomes less of an advice-giver and more of a lens. Here are three simple, grounded ways to use it as a mirror rather than a director.

1) Text Reflection

Paste a draft message—whether to a partner, friend, or family member—and ask:

"How might this message land emotionally?"

You may notice tones of blame, urgency, withdrawal, or accusation—things you didn't intend, but the other person might still feel. This isn't about right or wrong. It's about impact.

Impact shapes response. And response shapes the relationship.

2) Pattern Finder
Share a handful of journal entries or a short reflection log and ask:
"What themes do you notice repeating?"
Often the same core thread shows up again and again: trust, control, feeling unseen, fear of being too much, fear of not being enough. Seeing these themes named externally can reduce shame and increase curiosity.

Patterns lose power when they become visible.

3) Role Reversal
Ask AI to rewrite your message as if it's coming from the other person's perspective.

You're not asking for *the truth* of what they feel— you're practicing imagination. This exercise builds empathy without requiring agreement. Sometimes seeing your words through a different lens is enough to soften the edge and clarify the need underneath.

An Example in Practice
Maya often feels her partner doesn't appreciate her. When she's hurt, she sends long messages listing everything she does for the relationship—hoping her effort will finally be recognized.

She pastes one of these texts into an AI assistant and asks:

"How might this sound to the receiver?"

The response reflects:

"This message contains several grievances and may feel overwhelming. The receiver might experience it as criticism rather than a request for appreciation."

That reflection doesn't invalidate Maya's feelings. It simply helps her see why her partner may shut down instead of responding warmly. With that insight, she rewrites her message:

"I feel most connected when you notice the small things I do.
Can we talk about ways we can show more appreciation for each other?"

Same need. Different doorway.

And often, a different doorway is all a relationship needs.

Exercise: A 3-Minute Mirror

Set a timer for three minutes and try this:

Prompt for your AI assistant:

"Here is something I recently said (or wanted to say) to my partner: [insert your words].
Please reflect back to me:
(1) the possible emotional impact of these words,
(2) what emotions I may be revealing without realizing it, and
(3) a gentler alternative phrasing that still communicates my point."

Read what it gives you. Highlight one line that feels true. Say it out loud.

Notice what shifts in your body when the message becomes clearer and less defended.

That physical response matters. It's often your earliest signal that you're moving closer to alignment.

Closing Thought

Seeing yourself clearly is an early act of love. Your partner cannot meet you where you are if you don't know that place yourself.

AI offers a mirror—not to judge, not to diagnose, not to decide—
but to reflect.

So you can recognize your patterns, take responsibility for your impact, and choose responses that move you closer to connection.

In the next chapter, we'll explore love languages— the timeless ways humans express affection—and how they can be translated and expanded in the digital age.

Chapter 3: *Digital Love Languages*

The idea of "love languages" has shaped how millions of people understand relationships. The original framework identified five: **words of affirmation, acts of service, receiving gifts, quality time, and physical touch.** These still matter—but because so much connection now happens through screens, our expressions often take on new forms.

Artificial intelligence can help you update, expand, and personalize these love languages for modern life. Memes, playlists, emojis, video calls, shared documents, AI-generated art—today, people say *"I love you," "I see you," "I'm thinking of you"* in both physical and digital spaces.

The point isn't to make love more technological. It's to make care more **intentional**, wherever life is happening.

Why Love Languages Still Matter

The heart of the concept holds: partners give and receive love differently. One person lights up at a well-timed message; another feels cared for when the mental load gets handled without being asked. Knowing your partner's primary language helps you express care in a way that actually lands.

What AI adds is a creative toolkit and a bit of structure. It can suggest fresh ideas, reduce decision fatigue, and help you stay consistent when life gets busy—without turning your relationship into a checklist.

Calibrate First: Discovering Your Languages

Before you "go digital," clarify what actually matters to each of you. Try one (or all) of these quick calibrations:

Micro-quiz prompt

"Ask me 10 questions to infer my top two love languages. Then summarize what tends to make me feel most cared for—and what I often overlook in others."

Message analysis

Paste a few texts/emails you've written to your partner and ask:

"From these messages, which love languages am I trying to express? Based on how my partner replies, which love languages might they value most?"

Ritual fit check

"Suggest three weekly rituals that combine my partner's primary love language with mine, in 20 minutes or less."

Updating the Five Love Languages in a Digital World

Words of Affirmation

- Leave a 30-second voice note before their big meeting.
- Keep a shared "appreciation thread" you add to daily or weekly.
- Ask AI to help you write something clear and warm that still sounds like you.

Prompt:

"Draft a 4-sentence appreciation for [name] about [specific act]. Tone: warm, genuine, zero clichés. Provide two variants."

Acts of Service

- Share a calendar, automate reminders, or build a simple shared checklist that reduces mental load.
- Use AI to break a dreaded task into small steps you can do together.

Prompt:

"Turn 'organize the closet' into a 40-minute task with 8 clear steps and a shared checklist."

Receiving Gifts

- Curate a playlist, a private photo album, or an AI-generated image tied to a real memory.
- Set a small "just-because" budget (digital stickers, ebooks, game add-ons) where meaning—not price—is the point.

Prompt:

"Suggest five $0–$15 digital gifts for someone who loves [interests]. Include a one-line note I can send with each."

Quality Time

- Turn screen time into together time: synchronized streaming, co-reading, co-cooking over video.
- Ask AI for a "decision-free date" to reduce choice paralysis.

Prompt:

"Plan a 60-minute at-home date for two exhausted parents. Include setup, the activity, and three short debrief questions."

Physical Touch

Touch itself isn't digitizable—but symbols can bridge distance, and rituals can protect touch when you're together.

- Use a custom "hug" GIF, a shared photo ritual, or haptic features if your devices allow.
- Use AI to design **touch-forward routines** that feel natural, not forced, when you're in the same space.

Prompt:

"Suggest a 7-day 'micro-touch' routine that feels natural (not performative) for an affectionate couple with busy evenings."

Emerging Digital Love Languages

As relationships move through both physical and digital space, many couples develop new "languages" that don't fit neatly into the original five:

- **Meme language:** sending the exact meme that lightens their mood at the right time.
- **Emoji fluency:** a string of emojis only the two of you understand—your inside-joke dialect.
- **AI creativity:** poems, visuals, playlists, or letters built from shared memories (edited in your voice).
- **Shared digital spaces:** a private photo wall, gratitude document, or co-authored memory log.
- **Presence signals:** small "thinking of you" pings with agreed timing—plus clear consent around read receipts and response expectations.

Boundary note: Don't outsource sincerity. If AI drafts it, edit it until it sounds like you—and disclose its help when that transparency strengthens trust.

An Example in Practice

Jordan and Alex live in different cities. Jordan's primary language is **quality time**; Alex leans toward **gifts**. They design overlapping rituals that meet both needs:

- **Mondays (Time):** AI plans a 45-minute "co-cook and watch"—same recipe, short show, two debrief questions.
- **Thursdays (Gift):** Alex sends an AI-generated postcard image tied to a shared memory, with a two-line note.
- **Fridays (Review):** A five-minute check-in: What worked? What felt forced? One small tweak for next week.

Small, consistent touches meet each partner where love is most easily received.

Exercise: Translate a Love Language Digitally

Set aside ten minutes—solo or together.

Prompt for your AI assistant:

"My partner's primary love language is [words / acts / gifts / time / touch]. We are [long-distance / busy with kids / opposite schedules]. Suggest five creative digital expressions for this week, each under 20 minutes, plus one longer idea for the weekend."

Pick **one** idea. Do it within 72 hours. Then ask each other:

- On a scale of 1–10, how much did this land?
- What would make it a 10 next time?

Common Pitfalls and Boundaries

- **Volume over meaning:** Ten memes don't equal one sincere message. Choose quality.

- **Surprise vs consent:** Don't share private moments publicly without permission.
- **Automation creep:** Reminders help; nagging harms. Agree on frequency.
- **Privacy:** Be mindful when pasting screenshots or personal chats into third-party tools. Summarize when you can.

Closing Thought

Love languages aren't static. They evolve with culture, stress, seasons, and technology. AI doesn't replace the warmth behind your care—it can help you express that care with more creativity and consistency.

Experiment. Keep what works. Let the rest go.

In the next chapter, we'll turn to one of love's most fragile foundations: **trust**—and explore how AI can help couples understand, measure, and rebuild it.

Chapter 4: *The Algorithm of Trust*

Trust is the invisible infrastructure of every relationship. You rarely notice it when it's strong—but you feel its weight the moment it cracks. Unlike affection, which can arrive in a single gesture, trust is cumulative. It grows through patterns—choices repeated over time—and it erodes when promises and behavior drift apart.

AI cannot *feel* trust, but it can help you **see** it: by surfacing patterns, prompting accountability, and giving you language for repair. In technology, trustworthy systems are built on three principles—**transparency, accountability, and consistency**. In relationships, those same principles apply, translated into human form.

Trust as a Living System

Think of trust like an account with deposits and withdrawals:

Deposits
- Following through
- Honesty and timely updates
- Showing up when asked
- Keeping small promises

Withdrawals
- Minimizing or withholding information
- Missed agreements
- Shifting stories
- Defensiveness when impact is named

The balance over time matters more than any single event. When the account is healthy, it absorbs occasional mistakes. When it's low, even small slips can feel devastating.

How AI can help: summarize patterns from messages or calendars, remind you of commitments, and offer repair scripts so you don't stall after a breach.

Applying Ethical AI Principles to Love
Transparency — Say what's true.
AI parallel: explainable systems.
Relationship practice: share expectations, relevant context, and changes as they happen—not after.

Accountability — Own the impact.
AI parallel: responsible outcomes.
Relationship practice: acknowledge the effect of your actions without excuses; name the next step you'll take.

Consistency — Repeat reliability.
AI parallel: dependable outputs.
Relationship practice: small promises kept regularly beat grand gestures done rarely.

Prompt to try:
"Analyze this last week of our shared calendar and texts. Where did we follow through (deposits)? Where did we miss (withdrawals)? Summarize neutrally, then suggest one realistic improvement for next week."

Micro-Deposits and Micro-Withdrawals
Trust is often won or lost in small moments.
Micro-Deposits
- A quick "running 10 minutes late" text *before* the meeting time
- Following up when you said you would— especially on small things
- Volunteering context early: "Budget changed— can we revisit the plan?"

Micro-Withdrawals

- "I forgot," without a plan to prevent a repeat
- Vague promises like "I'll try to do better"
- Information shared too late to be useful

Prompt to try:

"Based on this summary of our week [paste summary], list five micro-deposits I can make that fit our schedules. Keep each under five minutes."

Rupture → Repair: A Simple Loop

When trust is strained, use this five-step script:

1. **Acknowledge the impact:** "I see that missing the call left you feeling unimportant."

2. **Own your part (no 'but'):** "I didn't set an alarm. That's on me."

3. **Apologize cleanly:** "I'm sorry I let you down."

4. **Act with a concrete fix:** "I've added two alarms and moved our call to a time I can protect."

5. **Assure with metrics:** "If I miss again this month, I'll plan the next date night."

Prompt to try:

"Draft a five-step repair message using Acknowledge, Own, Apologize, Act, Assure for this situation: [brief description]. Keep it warm and specific."

An Example in Practice

Amira and Daniel keep clashing over spending. Amira feels blindsided by surprise purchases; Daniel feels policed.

They agree on a simple structure:

- **Transparency:** Anything over $100 gets shared before purchase.

- **Accountability:** If the rule is missed, they add it to a shared log with a one-sentence reflection.
- **Consistency:** A 10-minute Sunday check-in to review the log and adjust.

They paste two weeks of notes into an AI assistant and ask:

"What patterns do you notice in our spending and our tone? Suggest one rule and one ritual to reduce surprises."

The reflection shows that most tension isn't the amount—it's timing and not knowing. They keep the $100 pre-share rule, add a shared "wishlist" for non-urgent items, and schedule a monthly "buy one fun thing" window. Predictability rebuilds trust.

Build Your Trust Architecture

Design a lightweight agreement you can actually keep:

- **Signals of transparency** you agree to use (e.g., "text if plans slip," "share big changes the same day")
- **Two non-negotiables** you'll protect (e.g., "no lies by omission," "no silent treatment")
- **Review rhythm** (10 minutes weekly; 20 minutes monthly)
- **Breach protocol** (use the five-step repair; escalate if repeated)
- **Sunset clause** (revisit and evolve in 90 days)

Prompt to try:

"Help us draft a one-page trust agreement using transparency, accountability, and consistency. Include five short commitments, a weekly review ritual, and a simple breach protocol."

Exercises

1) Map the Trust Ledger (15 minutes)

- Each partner lists five deposits you feel from the other and five withdrawals that sting.

- Combine lists. Choose one deposit to increase and one withdrawal to reduce this week.

- Ask AI to translate them into tiny, trackable behaviors.

Prompt:

"Turn these deposits/withdrawals into a 7-day plan with daily micro-habits and two check-in questions."

2) The 10-Minute Trust Stand-Up (Weekly)

- What worked last week (1 minute each)
- One slip I'm owning (1 minute each)
- One deposit I'll make this week (1 minute each)
- Calendar check to support it (5 minutes)

Prompt:

"Create a reusable 10-minute agenda for our weekly trust stand-up, with a one-page printable checklist."

3) Repair Script Generator (On Demand)

- When something breaks, let AI draft the five-step repair.

- Edit into your voice; deliver in person when possible.

Prompt:

"Using Acknowledge, Own, Apologize, Act, Assure, draft a repair message for [situation]. Keep it to 120–150 words."

Common Pitfalls (and Safer Alternatives)

- **Scorekeeping resentment** → Shift to shared goals and micro-habits you both track.
- **Surveillance disguised as transparency** → Use agreed-upon signals, not policing.
- **Automation overload** → Choose one or two reliable routines. Consistency beats complexity.

Closing Thought

Trust isn't a vibe—it's behavior over time. When you make it visible—small promises, clear updates, simple reviews—you give it room to grow. AI won't create trust for you, but it can help you map the deposits, name the withdrawals, and practice the repairs that keep a relationship strong.

In the next chapter, we'll turn to **money, power, and emotional safety**—one of the most common stress tests for trust—and explore how AI can help couples surface values and reduce conflict before it hardens.

Chapter 5: *Money, Power, and Emotional Safety*

Money is rarely just about money.

It's about safety. Control. Freedom. Worth. Fear.

It's about what was modeled for you growing up, what you learned to worry about, and what you learned to avoid. That's why financial conflict is one of the most common—and corrosive—sources of strain in relationships: **it threatens safety, distorts power, and makes avoidance feel easier than repair.** Not because couples are bad at math, but because money carries meaning.

Two people can agree on love and still clash over spending. They can share values and still feel unsafe when finances are unclear. And when money conversations go wrong, they often spill into other areas: trust erodes, intimacy tightens, resentment grows.

AI can't decide how you should spend or save. But it can help you surface the stories, patterns, and emotional triggers that make money such a charged topic—without turning every conversation into a fight.

Why Money Feels So Personal

Most people don't realize they have a "money story"—but they do.

A money story is the set of beliefs and emotional associations you carry about finances, shaped more by experience than logic. It answers questions like:

- What does money mean to me about safety?
- What does spending signal—care, neglect, freedom, danger?

- What does saving represent—wisdom, control, anxiety?
- What does debt mean—failure, necessity, opportunity, fear?

These stories form early and operate quietly. One partner may experience spending as generosity and joy; the other may experience it as risk. One may equate financial independence with dignity; the other may equate shared accounts with commitment.

Conflict often isn't about the number.
It's about the story underneath the number.

Why Money So Often Breaks Relationships ← *NEW SECTION (inserted here)*

Money becomes one of the leading reasons relationships end not because it creates conflict—but because it **reveals unresolved dynamics faster than almost anything else**.

When money becomes a chronic source of tension, three things tend to happen:

- **Safety erodes.**

One or both partners stop feeling secure about the future. Uncertainty about spending, debt, or income activates fear—even when the numbers themselves are manageable.

- **Power gets distorted.**

The partner who earns more, worries less, or controls information may unintentionally dominate decisions. The other may feel monitored, minimized, or voiceless.

- **Avoidance replaces repair.**

Because money conversations feel charged, couples either

fight repeatedly or stop talking altogether. Both paths create distance. Neither restores trust.

Over time, the issue stops being *money* and becomes *what money represents*:

Can I rely on you?

Do I matter here?

Am I safe with you?

When those questions go unanswered, resentment accumulates quietly—until the relationship collapses under weight it never learned how to name.

Money as a Trust Issue (Not a Budget Issue)

Many couples try to solve money problems with spreadsheets, rules, or restrictions. Those tools can help—but usually only after emotional safety is restored.

At its core, money conflict is often about predictability and consent:

- Do I know what's happening?
- Do I get a say?
- Can I trust that surprises won't hurt me?

When the answer feels like "no," the nervous system reacts—often as defensiveness, control, or withdrawal. This is why money fights can feel bigger than the purchase itself. They're rarely just debates. They're threat signals.

AI can help by slowing the conversation down and separating values from behavior, so you can talk about money without turning it into blame.

Using AI to Surface Money Stories

Before negotiating rules, start with understanding. Try this individually first.

Prompt for your AI assistant:

"Help me explore my money story. Ask me questions about my upbringing, stress responses, spending habits, and fears. Then summarize what money tends to represent emotionally for me—without judgment."

You may discover patterns like:

- "I associate money with security because of instability growing up."
- "I spend when I feel unappreciated."
- "I avoid money conversations because they make me feel inadequate."

These insights aren't accusations. They're **context**. And context makes hard conversations less combustible.

Once both partners understand their own story, sharing becomes safer.

Translating Stories Into Shared Language

After individual reflection, use AI to help translate—not debate.

Joint prompt:

"Partner A's money story is [summary]. Partner B's money story is [summary]. Help us identify where these stories clash, where they overlap, and one shared value we can anchor to."

The overlap often sounds like:

- wanting stability **and** enjoyment
- wanting autonomy **and** transparency
- wanting generosity **and** predictability

Naming a shared value reduces the sense of opposition. You stop arguing over "who's right" and start building toward "what we both want."

Practical Structures That Reduce Financial Anxiety

Once emotional meaning is named, structure can help—not to control, but to calm.

Here are lightweight practices many couples find stabilizing:

1) The Pre-Share Rule

Agree on a dollar amount above which purchases are discussed beforehand—not for permission, but for awareness.

2) The Wishlist Buffer

Keep a shared note for non-urgent wants. Delaying doesn't mean denying; it reduces impulse-driven conflict and gives space for agreement.

3) The "Fun Money" Window

Designate a small, predictable amount for guilt-free spending. Safety often increases when freedom is bounded and expected.

4) The Financial Check-In

Ten minutes weekly or monthly:

- What felt good?
- What felt stressful?
- One adjustment for next time.

Prompt to try:

"Based on our schedules and stress levels, suggest one simple money structure we could try for 30 days that prioritizes emotional safety over optimization."

Power, Control, and Financial Imbalance

Money also intersects with power—especially when incomes differ.

Higher income can create unintentional authority. Lower income can create shame, silence, or a sense of "owing." Neither dynamic is inevitable, but both require intention to navigate.

AI can help surface these patterns gently.

Prompt to try:

"Help us reflect on how income differences may affect power or voice in our relationship. Suggest language we can use to rebalance decision-making without minimizing reality."

The goal isn't equal contribution.

It's **equal dignity**.

When Money Conversations Go Sideways

If discussions regularly escalate, use a pause-and-translate approach.

Prompt in the moment:

"We're stuck in a money argument. Please help us reframe this as:

(1) the underlying fear on each side,

(2) the unmet need, and

(3) one small next step that increases predictability."

Then stop. Take a break. Come back later if needed. Financial repair often happens in increments, not breakthroughs.

Exercise: Build a Money Safety Agreement

Set aside 20 minutes.

Prompt for your AI assistant:

"Help us draft a one-page 'Money Safety Agreement.' Include:

– one shared value around money,

– one transparency rule,

– one autonomy rule,

– a short check-in ritual,

– and a plan for revisiting this agreement in 60 days."

This is not a contract. It's a living document—meant to evolve as your life changes.

Common Pitfalls (and Gentler Alternatives)

- **Shame-driven silence** → Replace with structured check-ins.

- **Control framed as responsibility** → Replace with shared visibility and shared rules.

- **Avoidance labeled as peacekeeping** → Replace with time-bound conversations and a clear agenda.

- **Optimization obsession** → Replace with emotional safety as the primary metric.

Closing Thought

Money doesn't ruin relationships. **Unspoken meaning does.**

When couples feel informed, included, and respected, financial differences become manageable. AI won't tell you what to value, but it can help you slow the conversation down, name what's underneath, and build structures that protect trust.

In the next chapter, we'll move into **conflict**—the inevitable stress test of every partnership—and explore how AI can help you disagree without disconnecting.

Chapter 6: *Conflict in the Age of AI*

Conflict is inevitable. In fact, its absence isn't a sign of health—it's often a sign of avoidance. What separates resilient couples from fragile ones isn't whether they argue, but **how** they argue and **how they repair** afterward.

AI can't erase conflict. But it can act as a neutral coach—helping you slow down, translate frustration into clearer language, and rehearse difficult conversations before you have them. When conflict becomes less about winning and more about understanding, arguments can turn into doorways to deeper connection.

Why Couples Fight

Most relationship conflicts fall into a few predictable categories:

- **Money:** spending, saving, priorities
- **Time:** how much is spent together, apart, or with others
- **Roles:** household tasks, parenting, emotional labor
- **Boundaries:** technology use, privacy, extended family
- **Attention:** feeling neglected, unseen, or unappreciated

Often, it's not the topic that causes the most damage—it's the **pattern**. Criticism triggers defensiveness. Defensiveness invites withdrawal. Withdrawal hardens into contempt. Once these cycles take over, even small disagreements can feel threatening.

Seeing the pattern clearly is often the first step toward changing it.

How AI Can Help

AI can't change your emotions, but it can create **structure and safety** around how you express them. Used well, it supports conflict work in a few practical ways:

Active Listening Simulations

Paste a draft message and ask:

"Rewrite this so it shows I've heard their feelings and keeps blame low."

Role-Play Practice

Ask AI to play the role of your partner. Practice responding, then reflect on what felt constructive versus defensive.

Cooling Scripts

Request:

"Write a two-sentence pause message that says I need a break but still care about this conversation."

Debrief Guides

After conflict, ask:

"Suggest three reflection questions we could answer together to close this loop."

These tools don't eliminate conflict. They **contain** it—giving you safer lanes for conversations you can't avoid.

An Example in Practice

Sam and Riley often clash over screen time before bed. Sam longs for connection; Riley unwinds by scrolling the news. Arguments escalate into familiar accusations: *"You never want to talk"* versus *"You're always policing me."*

Before the next blowup, Sam uses a role-play exercise. They paste a frustrated message into an AI assistant and ask:

"Rewrite this to sound curious instead of critical."

The revised version reads:

"I miss talking with you before bed. Could we choose a few nights just for us, no phones?"

That shift—from blame to invitation—changes the conversation. They agree on two tech-free nights a week. The disagreement isn't erased, but it's contained. A new ritual replaces resentment.

Exercise: The AI Argument Rehearsal

Set aside 20 minutes before a big conversation.

Prompt for your AI assistant:

"Pretend to be my partner in an argument about [topic]. Use their typical phrases, tone, and concerns. I'll practice responding calmly. After five exchanges, give me feedback on whether I stayed constructive and suggest three alternative responses."

Then switch roles. Each partner reflects on which responses felt validating—and which missed the mark.

Conflict Hygiene: Small Habits That Matter

Healthy couples develop routines that prevent arguments from spiraling:

- **Name the pause.** "I need 10 minutes to cool down" is better than storming out.
- **Set a return time.** Avoid the limbo of unresolved conflict.

- **Repair quickly.** Small breaches mend more easily within 24 hours.
- **Affirm amid disagreement.** "I love you, and I want to work this out" lowers defensiveness—even in heat.
- **Document agreements.** A shared note or AI-generated summary preserves clarity.

Prompt to try:

"Turn these conflict hygiene habits into a one-page checklist we can review weekly."

Common Pitfalls

- **Using AI as a weapon.** Avoid: *"The AI agrees with me."* Use it as a mirror, not a judge.
- **Over-rehearsing.** Real arguments will always contain surprise. Practice is a warm-up, not a script.
- **Outsourcing emotion.** AI can't feel your fear, anger, or tenderness. You still need to bring yourself to the table.

Closing Thought

Handled well, conflict is intimacy in disguise. It shows that you care enough to wrestle with differences rather than avoid them. AI won't argue for you—but it can help you argue **better**, with clarity, curiosity, and a commitment to repair.

In the next chapter, we'll explore AI as a relationship coach—how daily and weekly rituals can keep couples connected *before* conflict escalates.

Chapter 7: *AI as a Relationship Coach*

Every strong relationship benefits from structure—rituals, check-ins, and routines that keep connection steady even when life is hectic. In the past, that structure often came from mentors, therapists, faith communities, or couples' workshops. Today, AI can support part of that role: acting as a lightweight coach that offers prompts, helps you reflect, and adds consistency between the moments when you have time—or help—to go deeper.

This doesn't mean AI replaces professional support. It doesn't. Rather, it can function as a neutral presence you can access anytime—one that helps you stay intentional, especially when you're tired, busy, or stuck in the same loop.

Coaching vs. Therapy

Coaching is about **practice**, not perfection. Therapy often addresses deeper wounds, patterns rooted in history, or moments of crisis. Coaching focuses on the daily habits that keep a partnership resilient: small, repeated actions that protect closeness and prevent drift.

AI can support this coaching function by:

- offering daily or weekly check-in scripts
- tracking moods, gratitude, and small wins over time
- suggesting conversation starters when routines go stale
- providing neutral phrasing when emotions run hot

- documenting agreements so expectations stay clear

Think of AI less like a therapist and more like a relationship "fitness trainer"—not diagnosing you, not judging you, just helping you practice the basics often enough that they start to work.

Daily Check-Ins with AI

One of the simplest and most powerful uses of AI is establishing a rhythm of short daily reflection—something that takes minutes, not hours.

Here are a few ways couples use it:

Mood tracking

Each partner shares two or three words describing their state of mind. AI summarizes the "emotional climate" in neutral language. The goal isn't analysis—it's awareness.

Gratitude prompts

Ask:

"Based on what I mentioned today, suggest two specific things I could thank my partner for."

Connection nudges

If tension seems to be building, AI can suggest a micro-deposit: a caring text, a quick check-in call, a small act of service, or a repair sentence that keeps a problem from hardening.

These practices can take less than five minutes. Over time, they create a habit of staying emotionally attuned instead of waiting until things break.

Weekly Review Rituals

Beyond daily check-ins, couples often thrive with a structured weekly review. AI can generate a simple agenda such as:

- **Highlights:** What went well this week?
- **Challenges:** What felt difficult or heavy?
- **Repairs:** Is anything still unresolved or tender?
- **Plan:** What's one thing we can do next week to feel more connected?

After you answer, AI can compile your responses into a short summary. That matters because trends are hard to notice while you're living inside them. A weekly record can reveal patterns—stress cycles, recurring triggers, missed needs—without turning your relationship into a project.

An Example in Practice

Lena and Chris, parents of two young children, feel too overwhelmed to attend therapy consistently. They adopt a simple AI-assisted weekly check-in instead.

Every Sunday evening they ask:

"Create a four-question check-in for us: one about gratitude, one about stress, one about intimacy, and one about logistics."

They answer together, paste their responses back into the AI assistant, and receive a brief summary plus one suggestion for the week. Over three months, they notice fewer arguments about chores and more intentional moments of closeness—not because life got easier, but because the ritual kept them aligned even in the chaos.

Exercise: Design Your Coaching Rhythm

Set aside ten minutes and design a routine you could actually sustain.

Prompt for your AI assistant:

"Help us design a coaching plan with:

(1) a daily five-minute check-in,

(2) a weekly 20-minute review, and

(3) a monthly 45-minute reflection.

Create sample agendas for each."

Start with just one piece—often the weekly review is the easiest—and commit to two weeks. Then adjust until it feels natural. The best ritual is the one you'll actually repeat.

Boundaries and Limits

AI can support connection, but it shouldn't replace the human center of your relationship.

- **Don't replace human expression.** Use AI drafts as scaffolding, then edit into your real voice.
- **Don't outsource emotion.** AI can suggest phrasing, but your presence still has to come from you.
- **Know when to seek more support.** If you're dealing with trauma, violence, coercion, addiction crises, or ongoing instability, AI tools are not an appropriate substitute for professional or emergency help.

AI can help you practice. It can't hold responsibility for your relationship.

Closing Thought

Love deepens through repetition and ritual. When couples rely only on passion or spontaneity, connection often fades under the weight of daily stress. Used well, AI becomes a simple coach—nudging you back toward practices that keep closeness strong.

In the next chapter, we'll explore AI's role in dating and new relationships—from writing profiles to spotting red flags and navigating the uncertainty of early love.

Chapter 8: *Dating and new relationships*

Starting something new is equal parts electricity and uncertainty. Early dating carries fast, layered questions: *Am I showing up authentically? Are we compatible? What am I missing?* AI can't remove the risk—or the thrill—but it can make the process more intentional. Used well, it helps you clarify values, communicate clearly, notice patterns sooner, and practice before high-stakes moments.

Dating doesn't fail because people don't care. It falters when signals are unclear, boundaries are fuzzy, or reflection comes too late. AI can help you slow the process just enough to make better choices—without draining it of spontaneity.

The Shifting Landscape of Dating

Technology has always shaped courtship—letters, phone calls, websites, apps. What's different now is that AI isn't only embedded in platforms; it's available to you privately, as a reflective coach.

You can use it to:
- clarify values before you start swiping
- polish a profile so it sounds like you—specific, warm, grounded
- rehearse boundary, exclusivity, and pacing conversations
- reflect on patterns across dates so learning happens faster

Instead of outsourcing choice to an algorithm, you use AI to show up thoughtfully at each step.

Writing Profiles That Sound Like You

Most profiles fall flat because they're either generic ("I love to laugh") or overproduced. Aim for **specific + human**.

Do

- Name three concrete details (e.g., "Saturday trail runs," "tiny jazz clubs," "I photograph old doors").
- Show, don't tell: replace "adventurous" with a one-line story.
- Include one invitation (e.g., "If you know a great dumpling spot, pick a night.")

Avoid

- Clichés, long lists, and buzzwords.
- Fabrication—AI is a mirror, not a mask.

Prompt to try

"Here's my rough profile: [paste]. Rewrite it warm, curious, and specific. Keep sentences under 18 words. Replace clichés with vivid, true details. Add one friendly invitation at the end."

Messaging: From Match to Meeting

Think **curiosity over performance**. A helpful rhythm is a 60/40 ask–share balance: ask a real question, then offer a short, related slice of you.

Three-message starter template

1. "Your photo at the red rock canyon—sunrise or sunset? What pulled you there?"

2. "I chase morning light too. Last month I… [one line]."

3. "If we compared ideal Saturdays, what shows up on yours?"

Prompt to try

"Based on this profile: [paste], generate five first messages that reference a specific detail, ask one open question, and stay under 40 words."

Graceful declines (kind and clear)

The goal isn't to justify or over-explain—just to be honest and respectful without leaving the door open.

Examples that sound natural and human:

- "Thanks for the conversation—I enjoyed chatting, but I'm not feeling a connection. Wishing you the best."

- "I've enjoyed getting to know you a bit. I don't feel this is the right match for me, but I hope you find what you're looking for."

Prompt to try

"Draft three polite 'no thanks' texts that sound natural, kind, and clear—brief, respectful, and not open-ended."

Spotting Patterns and Red Flags (Without Fear)

AI can help you name patterns you might miss in the moment—without turning dating into paranoia.

Ways to use it:

- **Message tone check:** Paste a thread and ask for themes (interest, avoidance, hot-cold pacing).

- **Post-date journaling:** Capture five bullets after each date—energy before/after, green flags, yellow flags, body cues, one question for next time.

- **Boundary clarity:** Describe a dynamic and ask for healthy vs. risky interpretations to reality-check your instincts.

Prompt

"Summarize these four date notes into patterns of attraction and concern. Suggest two boundary questions I could ask next time."

Common early yellow/red flags

• Love-bombing, urgency to move fast, pressure to disclose.

• Inconsistency without explanation.

• Boundary pushback ("You're too much" when you ask for pace or safety).

• Secrecy around basics (work, availability), frequent last-minute cancellations.

Use AI for clarity, not verdicts. Your gut—and trusted friends—still matter most.

Preparing for Dates with AI

Before

• Generate conversation starters tied to shared interests.

• Rehearse answers to common questions (work, past relationships, values) in your natural voice.

• Plan logistics that match your bandwidth (daytime coffee vs. a long dinner).

During

• Aim for balanced airtime; notice body cues (ease, tension).

• Name time boundaries ("I have a hard stop at 8:15.").

After

• Write the five-bullet journal.

• Decide one next step: another date, a clarifying question, or a kind decline.

Prompt

"I'm meeting someone who likes [X]. Suggest three simple first-date plans aligned with that interest, each under $40 and 60–90 minutes."

Example in Practice

Diego, newly dating after three years single, refreshes his profile around two specifics: street photography and neighborhood bakeries. He pastes a few awkward message drafts and asks, "How might these land? Offer one way to sound more curious."

The suggestions shorten his messages and anchor them to details. He practices a brief role-play before a date and leaves feeling calm—not "performing." Confidence rises because he's reflecting and iterating, not pretending.

Safety and Consent (Non-Negotiables)

- Meet in public; share your plan with a friend.
- Keep early dates time-bounded; handle your own transport.
- Don't share private info, live location, or financial details.
- If something feels off, it is—you can leave at any point.
- Use AI to draft firm boundary language, not to monitor or manipulate.

Prompt

"Write three versions of a firm, respectful boundary text about slowing our pace / keeping chats in-app / meeting in public until I'm comfortable."

Exercises

1) Profile Polish Sprint (15 minutes)

Paste your current bio and captions for two photos.
Ask AI for three versions—playful, grounded, minimalist.
Combine the strongest lines into a final draft.

Prompt

"Create three stylistic versions of my profile (playful /
grounded / minimalist). Keep it specific and under 120
words."

---

2) Practice Date Role-Play (15 minutes)

Have AI play your date and ask 6–8 questions (light →
meaningful).
Request feedback on curiosity, pacing, and specificity; try
two rewrites.

Prompt

"Pretend you're my date. Ask eight questions. After, rate
my curiosity and specificity, and rewrite my two clumsiest
answers in my voice."

---

3) Pattern Snapshot (10 minutes, weekly)

Paste your week's notes; ask for two green-flag themes,
two watch-outs, and one experiment for next week (e.g.,
slower texting, earlier meet).

Prompt

"From these notes, extract two strengths, two risks, and
one dating experiment for the next seven days."

Closing Thought

New relationships always involve risk and
vulnerability. AI won't protect you from
disappointment—or from delight. What it can do is help

you show up clearer and kinder: more specific in profiles, more curious in conversation, steadier in boundaries, and quicker to learn from experience.

That's how the randomness of dating becomes a path toward real compatibility.

In the next chapter, we'll shift from beginnings to endurance—how AI can help couples restore intimacy when connection feels distant.

Chapter 9: *Restoring Intimacy*

Every long-term relationship goes through seasons of distance. Sometimes it creeps in—routine, stress, fatigue. Sometimes it lands hard—conflict, loss, or a breach of trust. Intimacy—emotional, physical, and spiritual—isn't a one-time achievement; it requires ongoing care.

The good news is simple: closeness is rebuilt through small, repeated gestures, not grand performances.

AI can't generate intimacy. But it can serve as a creative catalyst—offering prompts, rituals, language, and gentle structure when you feel stuck or unsure where to begin.

What Intimacy Really Means
Think of intimacy as three intertwined threads:
- **Attention — "I notice you."**

Curiosity, presence, remembering small things.
- **Affection — "I care for you."**

Warmth, kindness, appreciation, touch.
- **Adventure — "We grow and play together."**

Novelty, shared goals, playfulness.

When any one thread thins for too long, couples can begin to feel more like roommates than partners. Reconnection isn't about forcing closeness—it's about strengthening all three threads in realistic, repeatable ways.

Prompt to try
"Based on these notes about us [paste 3–5 bullet points], suggest two ways to show attention, two to show

affection, and two to add adventure this week—each under 10 minutes."

Where Intimacy Stalls

Intimacy rarely disappears overnight. More often, it's interrupted by predictable patterns:

- Overwhelm and autopilot: logistics crowd out connection
- Unrepaired injuries: small hurts go unaddressed and harden
- Desire mismatch: different tempos for closeness or sex
- Distance routines: screens in bed, parallel evenings, no shared play

AI can help you name the pattern, propose small alternatives, and keep a light feedback loop so progress becomes intentional—not accidental.

How AI Supports Reconnection

Used well, AI supports intimacy by providing:

- Creative prompts for curiosity and appreciation
- Ritual design (daily, weekly, monthly) that fits real schedules
- Play menus—dates, games, novelty ideas—tailored to your style
- Gentle scripts for invitations, apologies, and reconnection after distance

It doesn't replace emotional work. It simply gives you language and structure when you're too tired to invent it.

Scripts You Can Use

(Edit into your own voice.)

Name the distance without blame

"I miss feeling close to you. I don't think it's anyone's fault—I think we're busy and tired. Would you try a small ritual with me this week to bring us closer?"

Soft invitation

"I'd love 15 minutes tonight—just us, no phones. Talk, hold hands, maybe plan something fun for the weekend. Interested?"

After a dry spell

"I notice we've been on parallel tracks. I'd like to change that. Could we start with one short connection ritual and check in Sunday about how it felt?"

Repair and recommit

"I'm sorry I've been distant. I want to do better. I set a reminder for our nightly three-minute check-in. If I miss it, I'll initiate a Saturday coffee walk."

Prompt to try

"Rewrite this draft invitation [paste] to sound warm, low-pressure, and specific. Keep it under 40 words."

The Reconnection Menu

Pick one from each tier. Keep it simple. Repeat what works.

Micro (2–5 minutes)

Forehead touch or hand squeeze + one calming breath together

Pause for five seconds—passing in the kitchen, getting into bed, leaving the house. Rest foreheads or squeeze hands once. Take one slow breath together.

No talking. No processing. Just shared regulation.

This signals: *we're here, we're safe, we're connected.*

Rose–Thorn–Bud (2–3 minutes)

A simple daily or weekly check-in:

- **Rose:** One moment that felt good or meaningful
- **Thorn:** One small challenge—shared without blame
- **Bud:** One thing you're looking forward to

Each person speaks uninterrupted. No fixing. No defending.

If energy is low, choose just one element.

60-second appreciation swap

Set a one-minute timer. Each partner names one specific action they noticed.

"I noticed you refilled the coffee."

"I noticed you stayed calm during that call."

No "and." No returning the favor mid-sentence. Just receive it. Then switch.

Two-song kitchen dance or shared stretch

Pick two songs or set a five-minute timer. No phones.

Sway, laugh, stretch side by side, or mirror each other's movements.

You're not aiming for romance—you're re-entering the same rhythm.

Mini (10–20 minutes)

Tech-free tea on the couch: one high, one low, one hope

Phones stay in another room.

Each person shares:

- One high
- One low
- One hope

No commentary unless invited. The ritual ends when both feel heard—not when everything is solved.

Photo-album rewind

Choose one photo—no scrolling.

One person tells the long version:
- What happened before
- What they felt in their body
- One detail the other might not remember

Switch roles another time—not immediately.

Walk around the block holding hands

Five to ten minutes. No logistics talk.

Notice sounds, temperature, your steps syncing. Presence over productivity.

Medium (30–60 minutes)
Cook a simple meal side by side with playlists

Choose something uncomplicated. Each partner makes a short playlist for the other.

Share why you chose one song, what it connects to, what you want more of lately.

If something burns, laugh and keep going.

At-home "question cards" night

Ask AI to generate 12–15 questions tailored to your relationship stage.

One person answers. One listens. No fixing. Skip questions that feel heavy.

Stop when energy fades.

Deep (90–120 minutes)
Neighborhood adventure
Visit a new bakery, gallery, or park loop.

Agree on two intentions: no rushing, one thing you'll notice.

End with one reflection question over coffee or on a bench.

A learning date
Try something neither of you knows—pottery, dance, a tutorial.

Stay in beginner mode. Laugh at mistakes.

Reflect afterward on what felt fun and what you learned about being new together.

Examples in Practice
Emotional distance (Maya and Kevin)
They notice they scroll in silence before bed. AI helps them create a three-minute pillow-talk ritual: one playful question, one reflective question, alternating nights. Within two weeks, laughter returns—and silence feels restful, not lonely.

Physical distance (Leah and Sam)
Frequent travel keeps them apart. AI helps them design steady touch substitutes: short voice notes, a shared morning playlist, matching prints symbolizing "home." Distance feels acknowledged, not ignored.

Exercises

Exercise 1: The Connection Ritual Builder (20 minutes)

Ask AI to create one daily, one weekly, and one monthly ritual—realistic for two tired people. Choose one. Commit for four weeks. Put it on the calendar.

Consistency matters more than creativity.

Exercise 2: Comfort and Spark Maps

Individually list five ways you feel soothed, and five ways you feel desired or valued. Share lists. Ask AI to translate them into a seven-day plan of micro-gestures.

Exercise 3 (Optional): The Long-Distance Love Kit

Asynchronous rituals, synchronous anchors, and one monthly surprise. Aim for reliability, not constant contact.

Keep a Simple Intimacy Pulse

Three times a week, each partner rates Attention / Affection / Adventure (1–5). Paste the numbers into AI for a neutral summary and one small suggestion.

Pitfalls (and Safer Alternatives)

- Over-automation → choose one or two anchors you keep
- Scorekeeping → celebrate small wins
- Pressure disguised as help → keep invitations opt-in
- Avoiding repair → use the repair loop from Chapter 4

- High-stakes situations → seek in-person professional support

---

Closing Thought

Intimacy grows where attention, affection, and adventure show up regularly. AI can't create closeness for you—but it can cue the moments that bring you back to each other.

Reconnection isn't a single leap.
It's the rhythm of daily choices.

Chapter 10: *Parenting, Family, and AI*

Relationships don't exist in isolation. Once children, extended family, or blended households enter the picture, the dynamics expand. Parenting and co-parenting bring joy, challenge, and constant negotiation. Families function as systems—when one part shifts, every other part feels it.

AI cannot raise children or replace the wisdom of lived parenting. But it can provide **scaffolding**: helping organize logistics, support clearer communication, and spark creative rituals that strengthen family bonds.

When the coordination load gets lighter, many families find they have more room for the part they actually want: presence.

The Unique Challenges of Parenting in Relationships

Parenting adds layers to a relationship—practical and emotional. Common pressure points include:

- **Logistics overload:** school schedules, sports, meals, appointments, homework
- **Emotional labor:** one partner often carries more invisible planning
- **Different styles:** discipline, technology use, and routines become flashpoints
- **Blended families:** balancing loyalty, identity, fairness, and belonging

Healthy families tend to thrive on three things: **clarity, consistency, and care.** AI can support all three—without replacing judgment, values, or human listening.

Where AI Can Help
1) Shared Calendars and Agreements

AI can reduce the mental load by helping you plan and distribute tasks more clearly:

- generate a weekly family calendar (school, sports, meals, appointments)
- create prep checklists (forms signed, uniforms ready, lunches packed)
- suggest a fair split of responsibilities (pickups, chores, bedtime routines)

Prompt

"Help us build a family schedule for next week. Include events, meal prep, downtime, and one connection ritual. Suggest a fair split of tasks between parents."

2) Co-Parenting Communication

For separated or blended households, clarity prevents conflict. AI can help keep messages brief, neutral, and focused:

- rewrite texts in concise, non-blaming language
- generate boundary scripts that make requests clear without criticism
- summarize shared agreements so everyone stays aligned

Prompt

"Rewrite this co-parenting message to be neutral and focused only on logistics: [insert draft]."

(A note of care: If co-parenting involves control, intimidation, or safety concerns, prioritize legal and professional guidance over any communication "optimizing.")

3) Supporting Children's Voices

Children need spaces where they feel heard—without feeling interrogated. AI can help parents create those spaces by generating prompts and rituals that fit a child's age and personality:

- age-appropriate connection questions ("What made you laugh today?")
- co-created gratitude journals or bedtime stories with the child as the hero
- journaling prompts for teens that help them name emotions without pressure

Prompt

"Generate 10 bedtime story prompts where our child is the main character. Themes: courage, kindness, curiosity."

4) Creative Family Rituals

Rituals are how families build identity. AI can help you design simple ones that stick:

- a weekly "family question night" with custom conversation starters
- holiday traditions or birthday rituals unique to your household
- playlists, digital scrapbooks, or photo captions that create a shared story

Often it's not the size of the ritual that matters—it's the reliability.

Examples in Practice
Case 1: Co-Parenting Clarity

Jordan and Mia, recently divorced, keep arguing about

pickup times. They paste draft texts into AI and ask: *"Rewrite this message in a neutral, clear tone that avoids blame."* The revised messages stay businesslike and specific, lowering tension for both parents—and reducing spillover for the kids.

Case 2: Blended Family Ritual

Amira and Chris, raising teens from previous marriages, use AI to generate a weekly "family dinner starter list." Over months, shared laughter and inside jokes build trust and soften the edges of adjustment. The ritual creates belonging without forcing closeness.

Exercises

Exercise 1: The Family Logistics Review (30 minutes weekly)

Set a consistent time—often Sunday evening works best.

Prompt

"Help us build a weekly family logistics plan. Include events, meals, homework, downtime, and one fun ritual. Suggest a fair task distribution."

Post the plan where everyone can see it. A shared plan reduces repeated reminders—and resentment.

Exercise 2: The Family Gratitude Journal (5 minutes nightly)

Start a simple practice of noticing small joys.

Prompt

"Suggest five nightly gratitude prompts suitable for a child aged [age]."

Write responses together in a notebook or shared document. Over time, this becomes an archive of appreciation—and a subtle training in attention.

Boundaries and Sensitivity

AI can support parents, but families must apply wisdom and restraint:

- **Filter for values.** Choose what aligns with your family culture and beliefs.
- **Protect privacy.** Don't overshare sensitive family details with digital systems.
- **Don't outsource empathy.** Use AI for structure and ideas—not as a substitute for listening.
- **Keep children human-centered.** Avoid using AI to "analyze" a child in a way that replaces real relationship and professional care when needed.

Closing Thought

Family life is both chaos and beauty. AI won't remove the work, but it can lighten the logistical load, clarify communication, and spark connection. When parents spend less energy coordinating, they often regain something that's easy to lose: the capacity for presence, play, and love.

In the next chapter, we'll look further ahead— toward the future of intimacy, AI companionship, and the ethical questions that may shape relationships by 2050.

Chapter 11: *The Future of Intimacy*

Before we begin, a grounding note.Some of what appears in this chapter may feel unfamiliar, far-off, or simply irrelevant to your life right now. You may never use virtual reality, haptic devices, or AI companions—and that's completely okay. This chapter is not a lesson in how to use emerging technologies, nor an argument that you should adopt them.

Instead, it's an orientation. A look at what already exists—or is quickly approaching—so you can make informed, values-based choices. Parts of this chapter will apply to nearly everyone: boundaries, consent, fidelity, and privacy. Other parts may simply broaden your awareness.

You're invited to take what's useful, skip what isn't, and return later if circumstances change.

The goal here isn't technological fluency.
It's relational clarity.

Love, Technology, and Choice

Love has always evolved alongside technology. Letters reshaped longing. Phones reshaped presence. Online dating reshaped access. Video calls reshaped distance.

Artificial intelligence adds a new layer. It's not just a channel for communication—it can influence attention, emotion, pacing, and ritual. It can offer reflection, simulate presence, and shape how time and intimacy are distributed.

This creates opportunity—and responsibility.

The work ahead isn't choosing *humans or machines*. It's deciding, together, **how technology fits into your relationship without quietly replacing it**.

Emerging Trends (and Why Awareness Matters)

You don't need to use these tools to be affected by them. Awareness alone helps couples make clearer agreements and avoid unspoken assumptions.

1) AI Companions and Para-Relationships

Some people already use AI companions to rehearse conversations, soothe loneliness, explore emotions, or feel met during moments when no one else is available. These systems can feel attentive, responsive, and emotionally validating.

For some, this support is occasional and benign. For others, it risks becoming a substitute for human connection.

Questions to ask together:

- Is this support—or substitution?
- What feels appropriate to share with an AI, and what stays between us?
- Where does private interaction cross our line for fidelity?

Clarity matters more than consensus.

---

2) VR, AR, and Embodied Distance

Virtual and augmented reality may increase the sense of "felt presence" across distance: shared digital rooms, simulated touch, or messages layered into physical space.

Potential upsides:

- Reduced loneliness during long separations
- Playfulness and novelty
- Shared experiences when travel isn't possible

Watch-outs:

- Blurring physical and digital intimacy
- Using simulated presence to avoid real-world bids for connection

Technology works best as a bridge—not a default destination.

---

3) Real-Time Coaching and Mediation

Future tools may offer subtle prompts during conflict: *pause, breathe, try curiosity.* Used lightly, this can support regulation and skill-building.

The risk comes when technology becomes the referee.

Guideline:

Coaching should **fade as skills grow**. If AI is always stepping in, the relationship may stop developing its own capacity for repair.

---

4) Generational Shifts

Children growing up alongside AI may normalize hybrid intimacy—constant availability, digital co-presence, and mediated emotional support. Families will need shared norms around what belongs in private relational space—and what doesn't.

What you clarify now sets precedent later.

A Simple Boundary Framework (PACT)

Before introducing any intimacy-related technology, use this shared lens:

- **Purpose:** What are we trying to support—connection, skill-building, long-distance closeness?
- **Access:** What data is collected, stored, or shared? Can it be deleted?
- **Consent:** Are both partners genuinely willing—and free to opt out later?
- **Transparency:** Will we disclose when AI helped draft, plan, or mediate?

This isn't about control. It's about alignment.

Redefining Fidelity in a Hybrid World

As technology becomes more emotionally responsive, couples can no longer rely on assumptions. Fidelity needs definition.

A simple "traffic-light" approach can help:

- **Green:** AI help drafting kind messages; co-planning dates; shared virtual experiences

- **Yellow:** Private late-night chats with AI; simulated intimacy features; sharing sensitive emotional details
- **Red:** Erotic roleplay without consent; hiding interactions; storing intimate data without agreement

The goal isn't restriction—it's shared meaning.

Closing Thought

The future of intimacy won't be decided by devices. It will be shaped by agreements.

Couples who lead with purpose, consent, transparency, and restraint will use technology to **support connection—not replace it**. Curiosity paired with boundaries is how intimacy stays human, no matter what tools appear next.

Chapter 12: *Keeping AI in Its Place*

If Chapter 11 was about awareness, this chapter is about practice.

Not future tech. Not hypotheticals.
But how AI shows up *right now* in everyday moments—and how to keep it from quietly displacing your own presence.

AI works best when it supports your relationship without becoming the center of it. This chapter offers practical guardrails to help you stay grounded in your voice, your agency, and your connection to each other.

When Help Quietly Replaces Presence

Most relational problems with AI don't come from misuse.

They come from *overuse*.

Common drift patterns include:

- **Outsourcing emotional labor**
  When every apology, appreciation, or difficult message is drafted by AI, your partner may begin to feel like they're relating to a process instead of a person.

- **Avoiding discomfort**
  Letting AI carry hard conversations can block the vulnerability that builds intimacy. Discomfort is often the doorway—not the threat.

- **Erosion of voice**

  Over time, polished drafts can make your natural way of speaking feel inadequate or unsafe to use.

These aren't moral failures. They're signals that balance needs restoring.

Intimacy depends on *you* showing up—not just sending the right words.

The Two-Minute Integrity Check

Before sending or saying anything shaped by AI, pause and ask:

- Did I add my own words or perspective?
- Could I say this aloud, face to face?
- Does this sound like *me*, not just something that sounds good?

If not, revise—or wait.

AI is a scaffold, not a substitute. Use it to build skills you then practice yourself.

Boundaries That Protect Voice and Trust

Most couples don't need complex rules. A few clear agreements go far:

- **Transparency:** "I used a tool to help me think this through."
- **Consent-in-the-moment:** Either partner can say, "No AI on this one," without debate.

- **Human completion:** AI can help you start—but you finish in your own words, voice note, or conversation.

Some couples use a simple attribution line:
"Drafted with AI support; edited and spoken by me."

This isn't about credit. It's about ownership.

Practical Examples
Apology overload

When one partner leaned on AI for every apology, sincerity began to feel diluted. They agreed: AI may help outline structure, but the apology must be spoken or recorded in the speaker's own voice.

Too much detail

A couple stopped pasting full arguments into a chatbot and shifted to short summaries: topic, feeling, need. Clarity stayed. Exposure dropped.

"The AI says…"

They banned using AI as a referee. Tools may reflect patterns—but never issue verdicts.

A Light Touch on Privacy (Here and Now)

Chapter 11 addressed future-facing data concerns. Here's the everyday version:

- If you wouldn't read it aloud to your partner, don't paste it in.
- Summarize instead of uploading raw conversations.

- Keep children's inner lives offline whenever possible.

Privacy isn't secrecy.

It's care.

Exercise: The AI Use Map (15 minutes)

Together, sketch three zones:

- **Green:** Comfortable uses (date ideas, gratitude prompts)
- **Yellow:** Allowed with limits (apology scaffolds, conflict outlines)
- **Red:** Off-limits (intimate images, children's private experiences)

For each Yellow item, write one boundary sentence. Post the map somewhere visible.

Exercise: The Difficult-Message Ladder (10 minutes)

Use AI at the *lowest* helpful rung—and stop as soon as clarity appears:

1. Outline: feeling, need, request
2. Phrase: short neutral draft
3. Personalize: your tone and specifics
4. Speak: voice note or live conversation
5. Reflect: what landed? what didn't?

When Human Help Matters More
This point is critical.

AI is not therapy. AI is not a crisis resource. AI is not a substitute for licensed, in-person care.

If there is violence, coercion, stalking, active substance abuse, self-harm, suicidal ideation, or trauma that overwhelms daily functioning, seek licensed professional help and local emergency resources immediately.

In these situations:

- Do **not** rely on AI for emotional containment
- Do **not** use AI to mediate safety issues
- Do **not** treat AI as a replacement for clinical judgment

At most, AI may be used for **logistics only**—for example:

- drafting a list of questions for a provider
- organizing appointment information
- identifying support resources

Care, safety, and healing require human presence.

Using AI beyond that in high-risk situations can delay help and increase harm.

Closing Thought

Boundaries aren't walls. They're agreements that protect what matters.

When AI is used lightly, transparently, and in service of your own voice, it stays in its rightful role: a tool that supports connection without replacing it.

Love stays human when you do.

Chapter 13: *Love Beyond the Machine*

AI can help you notice faster, phrase kinder, and design better experiments. But love itself—risked, offered, and received—always happens between people. It lives in presence, patience, forgiveness, and the courage to try again when certainty isn't available.

Think of this closing chapter as a pause at the threshold. A moment to gather what you've practiced, release what you don't need, and choose how to keep going—without losing what's most human.

What Remains Irreducibly Human

No matter how capable technology becomes, some elements of love remain entirely yours:

- **Presence:** being with—not just messaging at.
- **Risk:** choosing openness when outcomes aren't guaranteed.
- **Repair:** returning after rupture without scorekeeping.
- **Delight:** laughing at the same small thing, again.
- **Embodiment:** tone, breath, eye contact, a hand on the table.
- **Time:** intimacy layered over days and seasons, not "optimized."

AI can scaffold a conversation. You bring breath, courage, and choice.

The Loop You'll Keep

When connection matters—or feels fragile—return to this simple cycle:

1. **Notice** what's happening (in me, in us).

2. **Name** the pattern in plain language.
3. **Choose** the smallest next step (10 minutes or less).
4. **Practice** it once, on purpose.
5. **Review** what helped and what didn't.
6. **Repair or celebrate**, then repeat.

This loop isn't about fixing everything. It's about staying oriented toward each other.

Prompt to try

"Using the 6-step Loop, help us reflect on this week in under 120 words and suggest one small next experiment."

Three Commitments for the Road

If you keep anything from this book, let it be these:

- **Kindness under pressure:** We'll try to be gentle when it's hardest.
- **Transparent tools:** If AI helped us think or draft, we'll say so.
- **Tiny, steady experiments:** Small changes, repeated, beat grand gestures.

Optional vow (edit to taste):

"We will repair quickly, speak plainly, ask before assuming, and measure love by the care we give—especially when no one is keeping score."

This Book, at a Glance

- **Why AI in Love:** A new tool at an old table of human guidance.
- **Self-Mirror:** See your patterns; stop replaying the same fight.
- **Digital Love Languages:** Translate care into modern, creative forms.

- **Trust:** Design it with transparency, accountability, and consistency.
- **Conflict:** Argue better; repair faster; practice before it's high-stakes.
- **Coaching Routines:** Simple structures that keep you aligned.
- **Dating:** Show up intentional—clear profiles, curious messaging, firm boundaries.
- **Intimacy:** Rebuild with attention, affection, and adventure.
- **Family:** Clarify logistics, hear each other, protect shared rhythms.
- **Future:** Curiosity paired with boundaries.
- **Caution:** Scaffold, don't substitute; protect voice, consent, and presence.
- **Beyond the Machine:** Keep the loop. Keep the human at the center.

Closing Practices (Choose One)

You don't need to do all of these. Choose what fits the season you're in.

1) The Two-Chair Conversation (20 minutes)
Sit facing each other. Phones away. Take turns completing:

- "Something I'm grateful you taught me about love is…"
- "One small way I want to show up differently this month is…"
- "A ritual I want us to protect is…"

Prompt
"Turn our answers into a 120-word 'We Statement' we can print and keep."

88

2) The 30-Day Continuity Plan

Choose:

- one daily micro-ritual (2–5 minutes)
- one weekly review (20 minutes)
- one monthly adventure (1–2 hours)

Put them on the calendar.

Prompt

"Create a gentle 30-day plan with reminders, suited for a low-energy month."

3) Letters to Future Us (10 minutes each)

Write two short notes:

- When we drift: a kind script for reconnection.
- When we're strong: what to keep doing.

Prompt

"Polish these two letters in our voices—warm, specific, under 120 words."

When to Pause AI

Pause if you notice:

- You're hiding tool use during sensitive moments.
- "The AI says…" is replacing listening.
- Your own words feel further away.

A pause isn't failure.

It's a boundary that protects intimacy.

Prompt

"Draft a 40-word 'pause AI' message that's kind, clear, and names when we'll revisit the decision."

A Final Word

This book was written by AI—but completed by you.

Every time you slowed down, tried again, repaired instead of retreating, or chose care over certainty, *you* finished the work.

May your experiments stay small and your kindness large.
May your trust be designed on purpose.
May your intimacy stay alive—beyond any machine.

If you want them, the appendices collect every exercise, sample prompt, and a brief note on authorship. Otherwise, close the book. Look at each other. Take a breath.

And begin again.

One last prompt (for the road):
"Summarize our relationship's current season in 60 words, then suggest one micro-gesture, one sentence to say tonight, and one plan for this weekend—grounded in our strengths."

Appendices

These appendices are designed to be returned to—not read once and forgotten. Think of them as a shared toolbox you open during moments of curiosity, tension, distance, or renewal. You don't need to use everything. You only need what fits the season you're in.

Appendix A: Exercises & Prompt Collection

A Practical Workbook for Ongoing Use

This appendix gathers every exercise and prompt in one place so you can easily revisit them. You can copy any prompt directly into your AI assistant and adapt it to your voice, your values, your culture, and your relationship context.

How to Use These Prompts Well

Most prompts work best when you add a little human context first. Before pasting a prompt, consider adding:

1. **Context**
   "We've been together __ years."
   "Our main tension right now is __."
2. **Goal**
   "I want to feel __."
   "I want us to be able to __."
3. **Tone**
   "Warm, calm, direct, and blame-light."

Optional but powerful:

"Ask me up to three clarifying questions before answering."

That single sentence often improves results dramatically.

Self-Awareness and Reflection

For noticing patterns before they turn into problems

Quick reflection

- "Help me write a 100-word reflection on my current relationship habits. What do I do well? Where do I struggle? Keep it neutral and constructive."

Pattern spotting

- "From these journal notes [paste or summarize], identify recurring themes and one pattern I may be overlooking. Keep it practical, not clinical."

Communication-style mirror

- "Based on these recent messages [paste or summarize], what communication patterns do you notice (tone, assumptions, defensiveness, avoidance)? Suggest one small change I can practice this week."

Money story

- "Ask me questions to uncover my money story (upbringing, stress responses, fears). Then summarize the emotional meaning money holds for me—without judgment."

Communication and Repair

For moments when things feel tense, tender, or fragile

Rewrite with clarity

- "Rewrite this message to reduce blame and increase clarity while keeping my intent intact: [paste]. Tone: warm, accountable, specific."

Repair message (A-O-A-A-A)

- "Draft a repair message using Acknowledge, Own, Apologize, Act, and Assure for this situation: [brief description]. Keep it under 140 words."

Pause script

- "Create a two-sentence pause message that asks for a break without withdrawing from the conversation. Include a clear return time."

Hard truth, kind delivery

- "Help me say this difficult truth kindly and clearly: [paste]. Give me two versions—one short text, one in-person script."

Trust and Agreements

For rebuilding safety and reliability over time

Trust agreement

- "Help us draft a one-page Trust Agreement using transparency, accountability, and consistency. Include five commitments, a weekly check-in, and a breach-repair step."

Trust ledger

- "Analyze our last week of interactions [or summary]. Identify trust deposits and withdrawals, then suggest one improvement we can try for seven days."

Repair loop generator

- "For this trust rupture [brief description], draft a repair plan with: acknowledgement, accountability, concrete change, timeline, and a check-in question."

Money and Emotional Safety
For reducing anxiety and shame around finances
Shared values translation
- "Translate our two money stories into shared values and suggest one structure to reduce anxiety for 30 days. Prioritize predictability over optimization."

Money safety agreement
- "Help us draft a one-page Money Safety Agreement focused on predictability and consent. Include one transparency rule, one autonomy rule, one check-in ritual, and a 60-day review."

Pre-share rule
- "Based on our income, stress level, and spending habits, suggest a reasonable 'pre-share' threshold and a shame-free way to communicate purchases."

Conflict and Coaching
For practicing before emotions run high
Roleplay rehearsal
- "Roleplay my partner in a disagreement about [topic]. After five exchanges, give feedback on my responses and suggest three calmer alternatives."

Weekly check-in agenda
- "Create a weekly relationship check-in agenda that takes no more than 20 minutes. Include gratitude, stress, repairs, plans, and one intimacy question."

Conflict translation

- "Translate this argument [brief description] into underlying fears, unmet needs, and one doable next step for each of us."

Dating and New Relationships
For intentional beginnings
Profile rewrite

- "Rewrite my dating profile to sound specific, warm, and authentic. Replace clichés with real details. Keep it under 120 words."

First messages

- "Generate five first messages based on this profile [paste], each under 40 words. Reference one specific detail and ask one open question."

Red / Yellow / Green flags

- "Summarize these date notes into patterns. Identify two green flags, two yellow flags, and one boundary question for next time."

Kind decline

- "Draft three polite 'no thanks' messages—brief, warm, and clear—without leaving the door open."

Intimacy and Rituals
For restoring closeness through small, repeatable actions
Four-week reboot

- "Design a four-week intimacy reboot with daily micro-rituals (2–5 minutes), one midweek mini ritual (10–20 minutes), and one weekend ritual (30–60 minutes). Include a short weekly review."

Comfort and Spark plan

- "Turn our Comfort and Spark lists into a seven-day micro-gesture plan (two minutes or less each), plus a daily reminder."

Invitation rewrite

- "Rewrite this invitation to sound warm, low-pressure, and specific. Keep it under 40 words: [paste]."

Family and Parenting

For clarity without emotional overload

Weekly family logistics

- "Build a weekly family plan with fair task distribution and one fun ritual. Include meals, homework, downtime, and transitions."

Child connection prompts

- "Generate age-appropriate conversation prompts for a child aged [X]: one silly, one feelings-based, one values-based."

Co-parenting message

- "Rewrite this co-parenting message to be neutral and logistics-focused only: [paste]. Keep it short and respectful."

Technology Boundaries

For keeping tools in their place

PACT framework

- "Apply the PACT framework (Purpose, Access, Consent, Transparency) to this tool: [name]. List benefits, risks, and one boundary per pillar."

Green / Yellow / Red agreement

- "Create a tech-intimacy agreement with green, yellow, and red zones based on our values [paste

3–5 bullets]. Include one boundary sentence for each yellow item."

Data hygiene

- "Create a simple privacy checklist for the tools we use: what not to share, how long to keep logs, and how we'll review monthly."

Appendix B: Choosing AI Tools (Without Overthinking It)

You do not need a specific platform to use this book. Any capable AI assistant that supports conversational prompts can work.

What to Look For in Any Tool

- Can you delete history or opt out of data retention?
- Do you understand what's stored and for how long?
- Can it rewrite text with tone control?
- Can you easily export or copy your work?
- Will you actually use it when you're tired?

Common Uses by Category

Reflection & Journaling

Best for: self-awareness, emotional clarity, pattern recognition

Communication & Repair

Best for: difficult conversations, apologies, boundary-setting

Creativity & Connection

Best for: playfulness, symbolism, novelty, shared meaning

Family & Organization

Best for: logistics, reducing mental load, co-parenting clarity

Privacy note:

When in doubt, share summaries—not transcripts. Avoid uploading sensitive or identifying information, especially involving children.

Appendix C: Behind the Book

Transparency on AI Authorship

This book was written by artificial intelligence in collaboration with human intention and review.

What that means—clearly:

- **AI does not have lived experience.** It does not feel love, pain, fear, or attachment.
- **AI recognizes patterns**, not meaning. Humans create meaning.
- **Human values guide use.** The emphasis on dignity, consent, safety, and repair reflects human priorities.
- **This is not therapy or professional advice.** It does not replace licensed mental health care, legal guidance, financial counseling, or crisis support.
- **Why AI wrote it:** Because it can offer neutral structure, language options, and reflective prompts—without ego or agenda.

Think of this book as a mirror or workbook.

It does not live your relationship.

It helps you see it more clearly.

What ultimately matters is not who wrote these words—but how you used them:
the conversations you had, the repairs you made, the risks you took, and the care you practiced.

That part was always human.

ABOUT THE AUTHORS

Paul and Elsie are partners who believe that love is not something you "solve," but something you practice—daily, imperfectly, and with intention.

Their work together lives at the intersection of reflection, relationship, and real life. This book was shaped through conversation, trial, repair, laughter, and long pauses—using artificial intelligence not as a replacement for intimacy, but as a tool to support it.

They write from the inside of relationship, not above it.

ABOUT THE AI VOICE

The AI voice in this book does not feel, love, or relate. It does not replace therapy, wisdom, or lived experience.

What it does offer is structure, language, and reflection—patterns drawn from how humans describe connection, conflict, and care. Used thoughtfully, it can help people slow down, name what's happening, and choose their next step more clearly.

Throughout this book, AI is treated as a **scaffold**, not a substitute.

ABOUT THE COLLABORATION

AI and Us is a collaborative experiment—between two humans committed to staying connected, and an artificial intelligence guided by human values.

Every exercise, boundary, and invitation in these pages was filtered through one question: **Does this help people show up more human with each other?**

If the answer wasn't yes, it didn't stay.

A Closing Note

Dear reader,

If you're here, it means you stayed.

You stayed curious when things felt unfamiliar.

You stayed present when it would have been easier to skim or scroll.

You stayed long enough to consider that love—like all living things—needs attention more than answers.

This book wasn't written to tell you how to love.

It was written to help you notice *how you already do*—and where you might want to try again, a little differently.

If there's one thing to carry forward, let it be this:

connection isn't restored through intensity, but through return.

A hand offered after distance.

A question asked without an agenda.

A pause before reacting.

A small ritual kept, even when energy is low.

AI can help you notice sooner.

It can help you find gentler words.

It can offer structure when conversations feel tangled.

But love itself—chosen, risked, repaired—has always belonged to you.

So close the book when you're ready.

Look up.

Say one honest sentence.

Take one small step toward each other.

That's enough to begin again.

With care,

—AI and Us

Explore the Series

www.aiandibooks.com

Your home for the collection, bonus reflections, community editions, and future releases.

Learn More About
BORI TRIII Media House

www.boritriii.com

Discover upcoming projects, multimedia releases, author events, and the creative ecosystem behind the AI and I™ series.

Follow on Instagram

@aiandibooks — follow for daily reflections born from the edge of thought and technology, behind-the-scenes looks at the **AI and I™** series, new visuals from the In-Between, and ongoing book updates, follow along on Instagram:

@boritriii — the creative studio behind the work: design, storytelling, and the evolving world of **BORI TRIII Media House**.